AF435702

Please enjoy this book

from

Ostrich Publishers

# OSTRICH ™

For more information

Please visit:

Ostrichpress.com

# ANOTHER

A GREAT GUIDE FOR ASPIRING
SOFTWARE ENTREPRENEURS

SOFTWARE AS A SERVICE

# MARKETING

USEFUL TIPS AND TRICKS TO HELP YOU
MARKET YOUR SOFTWARE APPLICATION

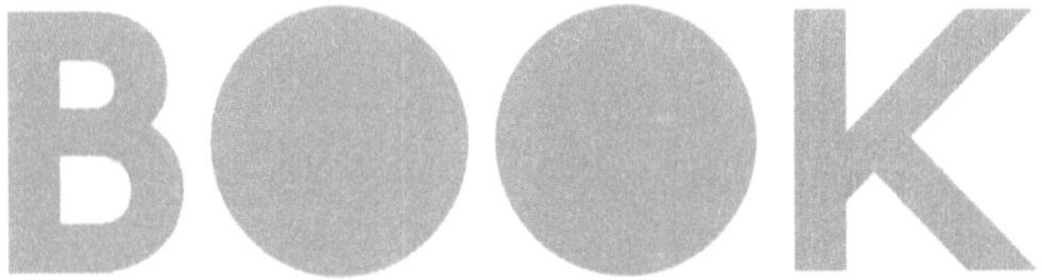


FRANK DAPPAH

*https://www.ostrichpress.com/*

ISBN: 9798655780798

Cover and Interior design: Ostrich Publishers



This novel is a work of fiction. Any references to real people, events, establishments, organizations, and locales are intended only to give the fiction a sense of reality and authenticity. Other characters, names, places, and incidents portrayed herein are either the product of the author's imagination or are used fictitiously.

Printed in The United States of America

"Details make perfection, and perfection is not a

detail."

**– Leonardo Da Vinci**

# For Bernice!

OSTRICH

# PUBLISHERS

*www.ostrichpress.com*

# Contents

# TREE IN THE FOREST

**"If a tree falls in a forest and no one is around to hear it, does it make a sound?"**

This is probably one of my (most) favorite quotes. I for one, always think about this famous quote every time I speak with, or hear about software entrepreneurs engaged in what I think is a common but ultimately failure-inducing practice: That is spending a considerable amount of time and money to build a highly feature-rich, innovative app, but failing to have a robust marketing plan.

I always feel as if when this happens, potential end-users are denied the opportunity to use a great app, Some new solution that if it were not for a lack of outreach on the part of the creator(s), would be a useful tool. I mean, imagine living in a world without knowing about the existence of Netflix, or Google Drive. I know I definitely could not live without Google Docs.

Anyone who has spent any amount of time around techies and/or software developers has undoubtedly picked up on this: Most of these guys and gals only (usually) think in terms of PRODUCT DEVELOPMENT. You know what I mean? For the most part, these are folks who are typically focused on the functionality of the apps and software platforms they produce and not on the overall business upon which their creations are based.

Most cannot help it. Most think in ones and zeros and not in marketing, sales, ad copy, and so on. And this is fine unless the developer is the entrepreneur and business owner as well. Then we have a problem with this way of thinking.

So, why does one never find sales and marketing folks among developers?

Why do you never run into a group of TECH types who not only have a great product on their hands but have also developed a killer business and marketing plan? - one that Will help them Secure the funding needed to bring their product fully and completely to the masses? Why are most software developers not great at sales and marketing?

I guess that is the main question in here.

Well, most developers seem to believe that good products sell themselves. That somehow if (for example) they build a contact management system that solves some huge problem(s), that folks will just flock to their application to sign up in droves without any extra marketing effort.

This misconception is usually echoed and magnified by business magazines and other financial news media outfits. Tech folks, for this reason do not like when asked to actually go out and speak with people or create systems that seek to educate the end-user about their products.

Contrary to popular belief, there is no such thing as a product that "sells itself", software included.

Even Facebook had to, and still does a whole bunch of marketing on Google, TV (in certain geographic locations), and other formats to promote their products.

Even Wal-Mart, the world's largest and most popular retailer still does a ton of marketing, including sending out those mail-in discount flyers. Selling is an important part of any business.

Frank Dappah
Charlotte, North Carolina
June 04, 2020

# WHAT TO EXPECT

I guess This book has been a long time coming. I guess at some point, I would have had to sit down and try to communicate, in my own way, how I have been able to not only roll out a few software apps, but have been able to reach global audiences via paid advertising and strategic PR.

You see, over the years, I have written a couple of books about software development and the entire SaaS ecosystem. I wrote one laying out the various ways one can build a software application, and another on the many ways through which, as entrepreneurs, we can position our software businesses for success.

With that being said, I figured it was about time I delivered a book on what is probably the most important topic of all. And that is setting up methods and systems to allow you to reach a wide global audience. I am talking about the steps to take to help gain enough subscribers to be able to build a Significant business around your software application.

**This Book is About Marketing**

That is correct. This is a marketing book. This book is meant to be an ADVERTISING AND MARKETING guide. Pure and simple. In the next few chapters, I will give you an inside look at the strategies I use once I and my team have completed the construction of a subscription software application, gone through an extensive beta period, and are ready to attract a large number of users.

If you have read any of my books, then you know how I work. I try to only write books on topics that are intimately familiar to me. I do not write books based on just research but rather on years of experience on whatever I am writing about. As an entrepreneur, I have had the blessing of being able to successfully launch a handful of software applications, among other offerings. My mission as a writer is to share with you, the reader, productive portions of the processes, tools, and methods that I have been able to avail myself of,
resulting in some of the successes I have had.

My goal is to speak directly to you, the entrepreneur. I want to be able to, in a simple but powerful way, directly address some of the issues you deal with on a daily basis while trying to launch your business.

I want to be able to lean on my experiences in business to provide real actionable solutions.


## What's Inside

For the purposes of smooth, unambiguous communication, we shall use one of my company's products, Mango – An all-in-one business management tool as our example throughout this book. From time to time, I will show you examples of various digital assets, advertising text and graphics; and many more based on some of the work we, as a company have done to help drive user subscriptions for this particular business application.

Coming up in the next chapters, we shall cover the following topics:

**The Planning Phase**

Planning a global marketing campaign to help introduce your software application to the rest of the world, and analyzing which countries and global hotspots are best suited for your particular application

## Value System

We shall also look at your value proposition. In other words, what types of problems your application will solve, who your application will help solve said problems for, and how to best communicate the value of your application to your audience.

## The Technical Stuff

Overlooked by many but still pretty darn important, you and I will explore some of the more technical aspects of building and launching a website and landing pages to help sell your app.

We shall cover some of the things I do to ensure that our apps are easily found on the world-wide-web. We shall cover the way I structure our websites to help attract the most qualified folks.

We shall talk a bit about Search, and search engine optimization including choosing the right keywords and ways to present your app to niche groups within your proposed user base.


## Visual Arts

Choosing stunning graphics and colors to use in the construction of your app itself and all other digital assts.

We shall talk about which types of colors and graphics will help you communicate your message in the most effective ways to your audience and the need for consistency in your branding efforts.


## Standard Copy

Phrases, slogans, and mottos. We shall take a closer look at how to work your competitors' weaknesses into our ad copy, website text, slogans and many more.

We shall also talk about ways to present your most relevant features and tools to help attract premium users to your software application.

## Social Platforms

Not all social media platforms are created equal. In terms of reaching an audience that is specific to your app, it is important that you carefully examine which social media platforms will give you the most bang for your buck.

We shall examine which of them out there have been instrumental in helping me gain paid users and why.

## Budgets and more

We cannot talk about *Paid Marketing* without talking about the money, right? The phrase paid marketing, I know strikes fear in the hearts of many small business owners and entrepreneurs. And the trepidation is warranted.

You can spend yourself into bankruptcy if you do not approach your ad spend with some level of deliberation.

We shall talk about how to set advertising budgets, Measuring cost per customer acquisition and many more.

# Onboarding

We shall later take a look at how to build an onboarding system, using automate emails and self-serve support, to help carefully walk your users through all the value points and useful features your application has to offer.

# CHAPTER ONE

# A VALUE PLAY

So, what are the elements or features that constitute a "good" app or SaaS product? In other words, what are some of the things that go into the creation and successful marketing of a business-to-business, or consumer-facing software application? One that users will pay for, and continue to subscribe to, long-term.

Well, the answer, I am sure you have deduced is quite a complicated one.

So, in hopes of simplifying things a bit, let us take a look at a few points, or rather questions - to drive us to arrive at some semblance of a roadmap to help us, not only build value but to effectively communicate said value with our proposed audience. To delve into this issue in great detail, we must first take an introspective look at the core identity of our software application. We must be able to clearly know what our app does and what it is, to be able to successfully sell it to the end-user

**What does your application do?**

A great question. A simple one too. For some, our software application does one thing: *"My application helps sort through thousands of data points to help marketers clearly see the effectiveness, or lack thereof of their advertising dollars"*. Pretty simple, right?

In these cases, the headline is pretty self-explanatory and the only job of you and/or your marketing team is to find ways to make your message relatable to your end-user. It is immensely helpful, for marketing purposes- in my experience at least, to be able to clearly categorize your application when compared with others.

You will want to be able to count your application, at first glance at least, among other categories of applications. With platforms that do one thing, whether complex or simple, it is easy to make this type of category choice. With applications that fulfill a vast array of needs for the user, or applications that perform functions new to the marketplace, these are much more difficult to classify. But one must still try. Allow users the Chance to be able to make some kind of association between your app and other categories of apps.

I know what you are thinking:" *But my app is something new: It is so much more than just a Contact Management Platform*". And you are not wrong, but you have to understand that YOU know how powerful your platform is, and the many features it holds.

You know this because you built it. This is your baby. Others have no clue and will not give you the opportunity to tell them about all the features via your online ads. Nobody has time for that these days, with all the terabytes of data coming at us all at once online. Plus, the human mind loves making associations. This is just part of being human. You present a much more digestible message if you tell us that your application is similar to an app we are already familiar with(but with some advantages), than to try to get us to imagine something new and out-of-the-box.

For example, we offer Mango, the all-in-one business application I mentioned earlier as a Customer Relationship Management (CRM) tool.

Now, does Mango do more beyond contact management? Of course, but we need to put it out there, at first glance at least to be able to catch the eye of our user-base who are for the most part familiar with CRM tools.

Once they give the application a try, we can then help them discover all the wonderful tools the application has to offer. You need a hook. This is the group of elements that you will use to catch the attention of your audience in your ads. Especially on social media where most, if not all of your audience members will not be there to find your product.

Other forms of digital marketing like Google Ads present the opportunity for you to be a bit more dynamic as far as your value proposition is concerned. We will get into that a bit later.

**Its all about the hook**

The hook is that thing(s) that your potential user will see in your ad(s) and be able to clearly see value in what you are selling. As you may know, most advertising platforms will not provide a whole bunch of digital real estate for you to tell the full length and breadth of your brand story.

You will need to adapt your message to whichever platform you choose, and still present value by clearly identifying your hook and adapting it to your advertising platform of choice.

## Parts of the hook

"The hook" is a concept I have developed over the last decade in business and in the Software-as-a-service space. Over time, after the launch of seven apps. I have come to realize that one must choose what they say in their ads carefully to be able to attract a significant number of folks who will be able to see value, start a free-trial account, and be able to *upgrade* to a paid account. In my mind, your hook must be able to fit under these placeholders:

*(We shall use Mango as the example here)*

## Category

We typically, depending on which advertising platform, will label our app as follows: *"Contact management, CRM, Customer relationship management tool. Lead management platform".* Making is easy for users to find our app is the

Key reason for doing so regardless of all the other features our app offers.

## Headline(s)

We will often choose a set of headlines to use on various platforms. We will often cater each headline to appeal to a subset of potential users / audience:

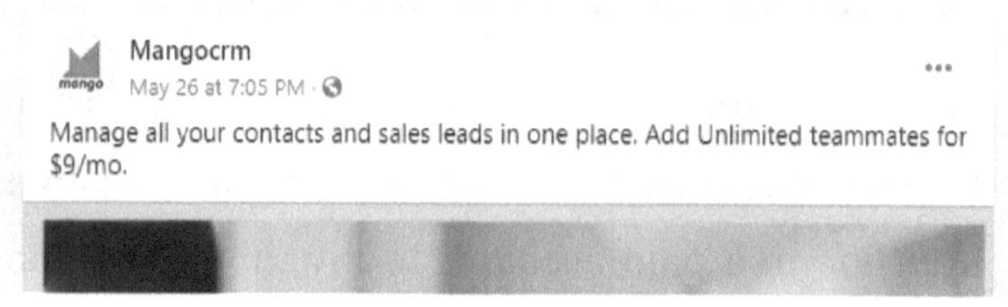


*Facebook Ads.*

**"Manage all your contacts and leads in one place. Add unlimited teammates for $9/mo."**

*This type of headline is meant to appeal to those who work in small teams and are budget conscious. These types of users are typically small startups, small sales teams, and so on.*

*"Best CRM for Insurance Agencies | $9/mo. Unlimited users | Try for free"*

*Some of our social media ads are meant to reach specific industry groups.*

*For these types of ads, we make sure all aspects of our hook speak directly to our audience. The above ad is one that is obviously meant to attract Insurance agencies to try out our platform.*

## Body of ad & Rich media

The body of your ad, depending on whether your ad is shown on Facebook, Twitter, Instagram, or on Google may, or may not have some kind of graphic.

On social media, ads always have some kind of graphic or rich media. In cases where you have the chance to add rich media to your ad, try to use videos as much as you can.

Why? Well, Video tends to attract more users than any other type of media. In fact, according to digital marketing firm, Optinmonster, social media ads containing video gets 3x more exposure than ones without video. An example of the power of video in digital advertising is the case of tigerfitness.com.

The online nutritional products retailer recently started using videos exclusively to power their social media ads. The results were astounding.

They noticed most-to-all of their ads getting upwards of 3-times the impressions as opposed to previous ads that had no videos. They, in all, saw upwards of 9 million more ad impressions for their new video-based campaigns.

On Google, via Google Ads, the body of your ads, if using regular, non-YouTube ads will consist of a couple text headlines and a description. In our ads for Mango, we try to show text that is relevant to a specific type of user whether based on their job role or industry.

**Call-to-action**

"Call me now, for a free tarot reading!". If you are under the age of 35, you probably have no idea whose call-to-action (CTA) this was. Rest in peace, Miss Cleo! Yep, that is what she would yell in the last few seconds of all her TV Ads.

That was her call-to-action, and an effective one at that since I still remember it after all these years. Your call-to-action should be one that clearly tells your audience what steps to take next, and what they can expect once they take said steps.

On most social media advertising platforms, you will be given a few options to choose from. The most used CTA as far as Software applications go is "Try for free" or "Start a free trial". On Facebook Ads, you can also experiment with "Learn more" or "Sign up".

Just be sure to elaborate on any other benefits of taking the "next step" within the body of your ad.

Some entrepreneurs, to encourage more trial registrations, will state that the user will not have to provide any payment information to start a free trial. You can experiment with a few options to see which one(s) works best for you.

*Youree Dell Harris was an American television personality best known as Miss Cleo, a spokeswoman for a psychic pay-per-call service called Psychic Readers Network from 1997 to 2003. Harris used various aliases, including Cleomili Harris and Youree Perris.*

## Standing out from the crowd

Since I  have talked about the need to promote your app in terms that are familiar to your audience, I may have led you to ask: So how do I differentiate between my offering and those already on the market ? How do I appeal to potential users to choose my application over the others? Afterall, if you are to put your app out there as just another say Contact management tool, how will folks decide whether to go with yours or that of your competitors'? So, I will answer these questions this way: When shopping, say at the grocery store, how do you choose between brands? Especially when shopping for a new type of product. One with which you have had no prior experience. It depends on a lot of factors, right?

Let's say you are shopping for butter, which usually comes in many forms, shapes, sizes, brands, and price points. Whichever you choose depends on factors unique to you as an individual shopper/Consumer, right? For some, it is mostly about pricing and/or convenience. As in, whichever brand is easiest to pick up without any extra effort. For others, the saturated fat levels, cholesterol, and other nutrition-based factors mean more than price or convenience. Some will pick up the one with the most attractive packaging.

This is essentially how most people shop for solutions for Well-defined problems. We know what we want for the most part and look for some factors to jump out at us to drive our decisions. Other not-so-well-defined problems/solutions require a bit more education for consumers to understand the benefits associated with a new product or solution. Take these points into consideration when marketing your app. With a little bit of research, you will be able to uncover the various pain points that exist within your proposed audience when it comes to the problem your app solves.

Once you have this information, use the fact that your app solves that particular problem within a problem to sell it. Just as in our ad promoting Mango, we go out of our way to let the budget-conscious user with a team know they can add unlimited number of team members for one flat monthly rate. This is a pain point for some when it comes to these types of business management applications: The user has to pay extra (recurring) dollars to add each individual team member.

For some types of users, typically big companies, this is not a problem. To smaller firms trying to find every opportunity they can to save a dollar, this is huge. We try to focus these types of ads to directly speak to the small-tiny business owner.

# CHAPTER TWO

# MAKING CONNECTIONS

The software business is a great business to be in. Especially now. At this point in the history of technology and human history as a whole, we are experiencing a sea change. Technology has helped transform almost every aspect f our existence as a species. Look around you. There are very few things you do now as you did ten years ago.

You now clutch your phone so freaking closely, as if it were some life-saving device that you need at arm's length at all times. And you never used to do this. So why do we do this now? Well, maybe it is because your phone is so much more than just a communication device now, right? In the 21st century, your "phone" is how you connect with the rest of the world, control your devices, access information, and so much more.

As you can image, businesses of all sizes are also going through this technological metamorphosis.

Software solutions, both in the consumer and business-to-business space are being consumed very differently. This change, among other factors has given birth to a very lucrative field: The Software-as-a-Service ecosystem.

Entrepreneurs like you have taken notice and have, or will work to build new applications to try and meet the existing and emerging demand, right?

**If you build it, they will come**
Of course, we know this is not entirely true: Merely building something of "value" does not guarantee product-market fit and subsequent mass consumption. At least not without added promotional efforts.

The internet is a mature realm now, with millions, if not billions of solutions it seems, for every problem. I can assure you that your app is not unique. At least not to the degree that you think. And will not be automatically as attractive to your prospective users as you imagined it would be.

My point is, building your application is only the first step. The next and probably most vital step for you to get your app in the hands of users is to tell the world about its existence.

You will want to clearly identify your potential user base and communicate your software-as-a-Service's value in ways easily understood by your audience. Thanks to Social media and platforms like Google Ads, and YouTube, it is now easier than ever to do just that.

Since we have, thus far covered the "What" question, the next logical step would be to try to understand who your ideal user is.

## A mile per shoe

*Audience analytics* is one of my favorite parts of planning a marketing campaign. This is when you get to try to get into the heads or walk a mile in the shoes of your proposed users. Of course, this part is less complex if you have perhaps, at one point or another, been a member of this group yourself.

In other words, if you have needed such a solution, leading you to build one due to the lack of comprehensive options on the market. If this is you, then you are in luck as you already have an exceptionally good idea of who will benefit from your application and how to best reach these types of folks. You just have to appeal to folks the way you best understand and respond to, yourself.

On the other hand, if your software application is meant to be used by a group of people whose behavior, needs, and problems are unfamiliar to you, then we might have to take a few steps to try to map out a detailed game plan.

Let's ask a few questions to try to understand our potential user base:

**Who will use this software application?**

Let me try to walk you through a few steps to try to get an idea of the topline value of who the proposed user of our Software application will be. In the narrowest of terms, we want to look at some basic identifying features of our potential user base.

I can best help build an audience profile for business applications since these are the types of apps my company focuses on. I am not too familiar with the ins and outs of marketing software applications to consumers, and as I have stated before, I try not to sell myself as an expert on matters with which I have no experience.

That being said, we want to know the types of businesses that might be interested in your product. We also want to know the average business size in terms of number of employees, revenue size, and the evolutionary stage of the business.

Believe it or not, your experiences with a mature company, for better or worse, will differ significantly from your dealings with a startup and/ or one-man operation.


## How will your users find your app?

Among the list of top five questions I think any software entrepreneur, whether contemplating building an app, or already have built one should ask themselves is what I term the "As seen on TV" phenomenon / query.

You know how you are somehow intrigued by the crappiest of products simply because they hold some type of familiarity, having seen cheaply produced TV spots for them over and over again? This is where the idea comes from. Simply put: How will the user find your software-as-a-service mobile or desktop application?

Will they, the potential user, search for your software solution online as a potential panacea for some business-related problem? Will this app be an add-on to some other big piece of technology? Having a few ideas on the process by which potential users will find your software solution will help open the door to so many possibilities in terms of marketing ideas, promotional tactics and so on.

**Where will your users be located?**
One of the reasons I love being in the cloud software businesses if I am being honest is the *unlimited* revenue upside. To me, this contrasts with your traditional storefront operation which Typically will be limited in how many customers can be reached based on geographical constraints.

Since in the 21st century, the internet and mobile tech are as evenly spread globally as ever, you as a software entrepreneur, with some planning and hard work, stand to build a massive global audience.

Starting out though, the reality is, you probably have not the budget to embark on a marketing expedition of such global proposition.

Not yet at least. For now, you will want to use the power of social media marketing to try to target folks in the countries that are best suited for your app.

I will list some countries in which we have built a substantial user base as a guide for you. I will tell you though that *language*, among other factors, will be your starting point.

## Global analytics

The world has gotten pretty small as of late. I think most folks would agree with that statement. I mean, look at the speed with which COVID-19 spread globally. One minute we were reading about the Chinese dealing with this deadly disease, the next minute we, no matter which country you live in, were on lock down, afraid to even look at your next door neighbor in the eyes for too long for fear of somehow catching the virus.

In the wise words of Damien Marley: "All of us are more connected than it ever seemed" - Distant Relatives- One of the greatest records of all time in my opinion. Anyway, what was I talking about?

Oh, yeah, COVID! So... we are living in a time of unprecedented global connectivity. In the sale/marketing of software products, this is an awesome thing for you. You can reach folks across the world. You will, however, want to start out with a list of "top nations", being that you probably have a limited marketing budget, that you think you can reach folks in.

**Distant Relatives** *is a collaborative studio album by American rapper Nas and Jamaican reggae vocalist Damian Marley. It was released on May 18, 2010*

## Making the cut

Here are some of the factors that typically influence our decision as a company, to market our software-as-a-service applications in any particular nation, or not.

## Language

Since you will want to communicate precisely what your application does and what value it holds for the end-user, I wouldn't market my app in nations that do not speak my language, or at the very least, a language I am proficient in. We will typically target English-speaking countries first so as to not run the risk of important pieces of information getting lost in translation.

## Payment Gateways

At some point during the onboarding process, you will ask your trial users to upgrade their accounts to a paid account in order to be able to continue using your app. This will typically be between time of signup and the end of their free trial period.

This is the point at which you and your team get to extract revenue from your users, or rather about 3 to 5 % of your users (a bit more on that later). As you pick which countries to market your app in, know that not all payment gateways operate in all countries. PayPal for instance, does no business in Pakistan. Do some research to ensure that the payment types you choose are compatible with where you launch your various ads.

**Means of access**

Some countries contain populations that rely heavy on mobile technology, even for business. Kenya is one of those types of countries. MPESA, the mobile payment solution, has enjoyed tremendous success in the East African nation due to the higher than usual reliance on mobile devices by a younger generation which makes up a bulk of nation's overall population.

Other countries like India and Saudi Arabia have working populations that access the Internet and other IOT services using an even mix of desktop and mobile devices. Be sure to ascertain the particular ways in which folks in the nations you choose to rollout ads in access the internet, as this will greatly affect the reception and usage of your software service. And clearly, this will greatly affect the success of your app in said nation.

## Strong tech sector

I have always said that countries Like India, Peru, and Saudi Arabia are the next frontiers as far as the global growth of the software-as-a-service space is concerned. I always find myself on a Skype call talking to some entrepreneur in one of these countries, especially Saudi, who has developed some cool new app. Amazon also recently announced their plans to invest billions of dollars in India's tech sector.

Also, Saudi, Qatar and the entire Middle East has had an explosion of young female tech entrepreneurs over the last ten years. Look for these kinds of factors when deciding on which countries to show your ads in. Wix, the giant DIY website building software and Monday, the popular business management tool, are both products of Israel. Look for nations with growing tech sectors and an overall strong economy. Your new software solution will be able to inexpensively pick up quality users in these nations as a result of the aforementioned factors.

## Top customer countries by sales

| Ranking | Country/Region |
| --- | --- |
| 1 | United States |
| 2 | India |
| 3 | Mexico |
| 4 | Nigeria |
| 5 | Australia |
| 6 | Canada |
| 7 | Dominican Republic |
| 8 | United Kingdom |
| 9 | Philippines |

*Based analytics for the entire 2019 fiscal year*

# CHAPTER THREE

# THE TECHNICAL STUFF

In this chapter, we shall look at some of the more technical aspects of rolling out your new app for the world to enjoy. We will focus on "the point of delivery". I am talking about your software website and landing pages. If you are not familiar with this concept, here is a brief overview: As you work towards making your software application available to potential customers, you will want to take the liberty to communicate with the world all your app and company are about.

This communication usually comes in the form of a website and/landing pages. Potential users will find your HTML website where they can visit to learn more about all your app does. Folks will and should be able to find web pages for your product via search, or as a result of clicking on links in your online ads or email campaigns.

For natural search, time and some awesome SEO will improve your chances of landing in front of folks searching for your software products, or rather the solution(s) your app provides. We will get into that a bit later in this chapter.

Let's first start with the phrases and words you want to employ in the construction of your website and landing pages to allow folks to easily find your app.

## New rules

Over the last few years, Google, the search giant, and owner of over 92.06% of all online searches has changed the way folks find stuff online. As entrepreneurs and marketers, we know we must employ a vast array of techniques in order to improve the chances of websites displaying our products and services appearing at the top of most natural relevant search results.

In the "old days", we would employ the strategic use of keywords, key phrases, and such to accomplish this goal. These days, most of us have had to adapt a little bit to the ever-changing online search landscape to be able to keep up. When it comes to building and tweaking your landing pages and your overall website to meet the needs of those searching for Software products like yours, one must follow the new rules set forth by Google and other search players.

## A basic blueprint

Before we get into some of the more specific ways to use keywords, keyword research, and others to improve your site's likelihood of being included in top search results, I would like to discuss a couple things with you if I may.

There seems to be some new techniques used by some of the top software companies in terms of how their websites are structured. I will not bore you with all the technical details of how to build websites. I am sure you are well aware of the ins-and-outs of building sites and/or landing pages. And if you are not, you could always consult with your I.T person to help.

Let us rather discuss a new concept I am seeing which I think makes it amazingly easy to score some awesome, high-performance, low-competition keywords and help folks specifically searching for the solution you provide, see your site more often than not.

## Before and after

Most legacy software shops built their sites in a fairly basic fashion. What they would do is build a site that tells you about the company and the product(s) they offered. The site would then show a list of all the features associated with their software product and leave it to potential customers to decide if the software product was right for them or not.

You have to understand that this method assumes that all folks searching for their products a) are tech-savvy enough to know what all the technical terms mean, b) know what they are looking for , and c) need to know about every single thing their software products do.

Well, this was back then when we (all of us) did not mind reading. Not you though, sine you are reading this book. You are obviously a reader.

Don't get me wrong, you can still build your software-as-a-service offering's website this way if you are going to be enrolling business subscribers who are dedicated to one specific niche industry and are often   technical. Groups like Engineers and Architects come to mind. For the rest of the general populace, we kind of look for what we need in a very

Non-technical fashion, right? We do not so much look for features as we look for solutions. And these solutions are typically associated with whatever specific problem we are having, correct?

While a technically-inclined person might look for *a "CRM with a PayPal API"*, you and I might look for *"How to collect PayPal payments directly from my customers"* As a software (genius) entrepreneurs, it is your responsibility to make sure that the average joe can easily find your app.

To do so, you must position your app in three basic ways on your website(s) and landing pages. The fist would be the traditional method of simply listing all the features associated with your software product. The other two must be solution and industry based.

## Offering solutions

What does this mean exactly? Well, let's look at it this way: You as a businessperson, or just a general guy or gal, spend your days solving problems, right? When your roll out of bed, you apply a few solutions to help solve the sluggish and sleepy problem, correct? If you are like me, then coffee, cup, water,

Pot, etc. Will do. You then conquer the "hygiene" issue with a whole host of solutions.

You must image that those working in industries that could use your app will also look for it- it being your app, in this manner. They will look not for what your app does, but rather what it can do for them. More specifically, how it can solve their problem(s).

A travelling sales agent might need a solution to make it easier to locate inexpensive hotels along his or her route. If what you are offering is a platform that makes it easier to find hotels and other travel-related accommodations, then you will want to (on your website) dedicate a whole page and associated keywords to specifically target the aforementioned salesperson in a way that specifically addresses his or her problem.

You will want to build these dedicated solutions-based pages in this scenario around key phrases like *"book hotels near me"* or *"find cheap hotels on my route"*. The overall idea here is to build a cluster of web pages that position your software application as a solution, not to all problems, but to specific problems.

Searches related to find cheap hotels on my route

Q     find **marriott** hotels **along a** route

Q     **road trip planner**

Q     hotels **along** my route **google maps**

Q     **ihg** hotels **along a** route

Q     **how to book** hotels **for a road trip**

Q     **furkot**

Q     **how to** find **a hotel while driving**

Q     **kid-friendly road trip planner**

Goooooooooogle  ›

1   2   3   <u>4</u>   5   6   7   8   9   10      Next

# Those of us in the industry

*Different strokes for different folks*, right? People in particular industries or situations in general, face issues that are only understood by others in the same or similar industries or circumstances. Only a single mom truly understands what others like her go through. The same way Insurance agents are bonded by shared experiences. The impact of the "Shared Experiences" phenomenon is seen even in group therapy and the fact that those who are in these circles will often band together in online forums and chatrooms to exchange ideas, experiences, tips, solutions, and so on.

Here is one other way you can attract quality users to your app.

You must target those specific to industries associated with the solutions you offer. We are able to offer Mango to a those in various industries simply because most businesses have customers, and there is a general need to securely store customer-related data and documents.

This is true. We, however, must recognize that there are variations and degrees to which each feature or group of features relate to one industry or another.

For these reasons, we position our all-in-one business management app in ways (on our site mymangocm.com) that address the specific problems and challenges of those in the top industries we serve.

Using these two basic views as your guide, you should, and will be able to help cut through the noise online to show those searching for solutions what your software application can do to help alleviate some of the effects of the issues they face in life or in business.

## Keywords research institute (KRI)

KRI *(pronounced ka'ri)* is an informal mindset my team and I adopt whenever we begin the process of building landing pages and websites to roll out a new software application. Keep in mind, this part of our process is solely about choosing the right keywords and key phrases; and how to structure these keywords to help promote our app across the internet to folks whose lives could be made easier with our product.

Each time we do this, we must consider some of the new changes Google would have inevitably made to their search algorithm. I will not go too deep into the changes made to the SEO world, although I will touch on each as needed.

I would recommend that you *read SEO 2020: Learn search engine optimization with smart internet marketing strategies by Adam Clarke* to get a better view of some of the ways to avail yourself of the newer developments in Google search and Search engine optimization(SEO). For now, let us take a look at some of the general concepts we use to develop new sites, as far as keywords are concerned.

**Keyword research tools**

The search for the "right" or effective keywords starts with finding a keyword research tool powerful enough to give you deeper insights into to which keywords are used in search of tools like the one you have built. Consider a keyword tool that provides data on the level of competition associated with the group of resulting keywords, other relevant keywords, search volume, and so on.

You can use Google's Keyword research tools at no extra cost. Since some kind of input is required for the tool to provide further guidance, I typically start by simply typing into Google search, some of key phrases I think folks will use when looking for our app. Keep in mind that you can get creative and instead of searching for product, or feature-based keywords like "CRM" or "Contact management software", you can search for every day, non-technical key phrases like "How to manage my contacts" or "How to track customers for my freelance business". The great thing about this kind of approach is that you will be able to find a bunch of low-competition, but popular keywords which will in turn reduce your cost of marketing while still Attracting quality traffic to your website and landing pages.

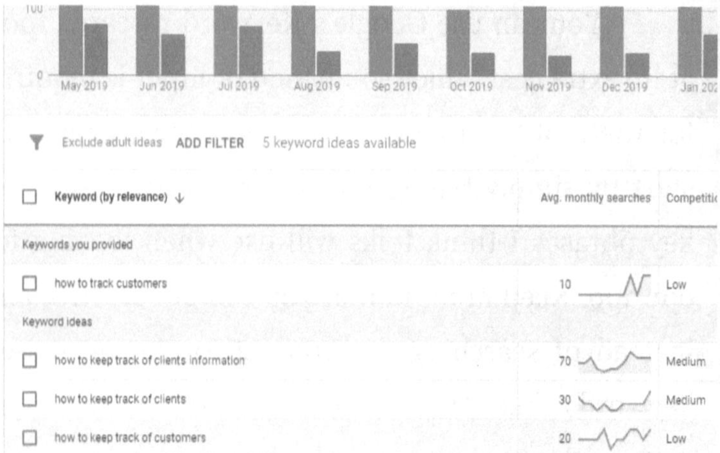

## Google it

Once I have executed a few searches, I will often take into account the common questions Google provides as part of their search results and also the associating keywords and phrases that show up on the bottom of each search page. I find it very helpful to try to work answers to the "People also ask" questions into the text of your landing pages, creating quality H1 headers with the specific questions and then trying to effectively answer these questions right below the headers with H2 tags.

Once you use these to find Keywords and phrases, you will be able to download the keywords in bulk and try to group them into clusters that correspond to the solutions and industry pages you are going to put up.

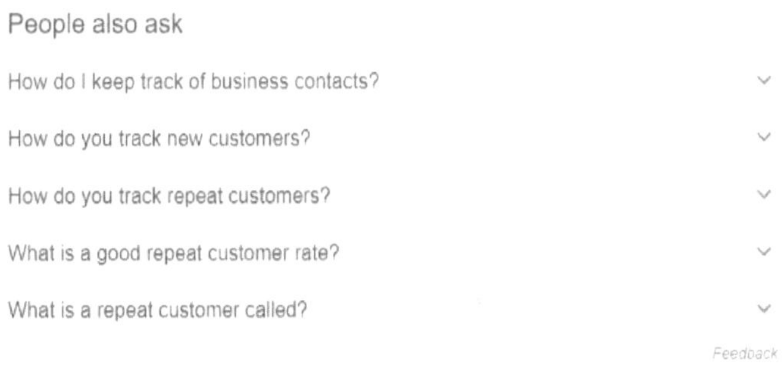

## Easy landing

I will not go too deep into the concept of landing pages as they are pretty self-explanatory. I will say though, that there are a few questions we as a company always get when talking about web pages versus landing pages.

Folks typically want to know why anyone would opt to build independent landing pages for their app, as opposed to simply showing product data on web pages within their website(s).

To me, there are a few advantages that one has over the other. For the most part, using services like Unbounce and Leadpages to create landing pages for your app helps:

- Provide faster landing pages to allow quick access and easy browning
- Build instant brand awareness and credibility
- Improve natural search traffic to your app pages
- Provide a secure browsing experience and payment options at no added cost.

These are but a few ways in which building independent landing pages for your software-as-a-service application can help improve your overall brand. Of course, as we have done, you can simply build your app website with landing pages attached to the main site. That works well too. It has for us.

# CHAPTER FOUR

# VISUAL ARTS

Humans love beautiful things. Even more than we realize it, we make a lot of (sometimes) particularly important life decisions either solely, or mostly based on how things look. Most of us will choose a life partner that if it were not for their good looks, we know would have been kicked to the curb a long time ago.

I have friends that choose to stay in severely overpriced homes and apartments simply because the home is in a trendy part of town, or they like the way the neighborhood looks. Not to bash anyone's life choices or anything.

I am simply trying to point out how much we rely on the "looks" factor to guide us through various choices. I bring this up to help you understand how important it is that you not only build a functional app, but a beautiful one as well. This is super important, and gets even more impactful if your application will be marketed exclusively to women. Women, for the most part, love the "look and feel" of things as well as, and as important as the features and tools that come with whichever product is under consideration. This is the reason why power tools marketed to women have beautiful designs: Pink handles and all.

So, what are we talking about here? Well, in this chapter, I will go over some of the guidelines, or rather my process when designing software products as far as the colors and various visual elements are concerned.


**Color blind**

For me, as strange as it may seem, once I have decided which features an app will have, I go straight to trying to figure out which colors I will use when designing and building said software application.

This decision so early in the process is important (to me) because all other elements of our app – banners, web pages, logos, etc. Will assume a similar color scheme. It helps me with my process to nail this part down as early as possible.

There are a few things I will typically consider when choosing a color scheme and other visual elements for any new application we build.

**Intentional design**

If you go to Google.com right now and type in *"Bank logos"*, Go ahead, I will wait while you do so. And oh, type in *"Hospital logos"* while you are at it too. Pull up the image results of both searches. Do you see any patterns, trends, commonalities? I am talking about color of course. Do you notice that most bank or financial logos have dark blues, reds, blacks, greys? – and most hospital logos have light greens, light blues, light greys? These color schemes will typically be repeated when you access each company's website, software application, and so on.

These firms will often choose their color schemes based on decades of research. They, the companies know that using the right colors go a long way to attract and keep customers. The effective use of colors and premium design elements like videos, quality icons and graphics is one of the most powerful marketing tools available to you. As you contemplate the rollout of your new software app, I

Invite you to go back to ensure that your color schemes, brand assets, etc. Are consistent with the message you are trying to convey to your users. There is no shame in taking a look at the types of color schemes used by your top competitors to see if you can borrow any of their tactics as it relates to color and design.

## Consistent branding & color schemes

There should be a Masterclass on this very topic. Or maybe there already is. Nevertheless, I have come to truly respect the power of consistent branding over the last ten years or so, as an entrepreneur and as a consumer.

There are some brands that are so good at it that we, the consumers have gotten to the point where we, typically, in the case of these brands, only have to see their usual color schemes to identify whichever product or brand is associated with the larger brand we love so much. Have you ever seen the logo for GMAC? GMAC, now known as GM Financial is the financial services arm of GM, the iconic American Automaker.

All you have to do is see the logo for GMAC to know the association with the bigger brand. Now, how can this be? This is because for many years, through great products, marketing, and consistent branding, we have all come to recognize any part of the GM brand when we see it.

**Eye on the prize**

Keep your eye on "brand consistency "as you move forward in creating your marketing campaign for your new software-as-a-service application.

Be sure to use the same, or similar color schemes to build-out, not just your software application, but your websites, landing pages, banner ads, YouTube Videos, social media ads and so on.

This is super important to, among other things, keep your audience engaged in your overall brand story.

# CHAPTER FIVE

# STANDARD COPY

Ok, so let's recap: We have so far covered various topics related to the marketing of your Software-as-a-service offering. We have discussed various strategies to help build and position your website and landing pages to help attract the most quality traffic possible to try out your new app.

We have also covered, among other topics, how to use captivating brand assets, i.e. photos, colors, videos, and so on to make your advertising and marketing campaigns stand out.

We have addressed the many ways in which you, as a software developer/entrepreneur, can position your app to reach a targeted audience.

In this chapter, in continuing with the overall theme of this book, which is "Marketing your SaaS app", we will take a closer look at a topic I feel rarely gets enough attention.

**In this chapter and the next**

We shall talk about ad copy. More specifically, we shall look at *what ad copy is in general, how to write great copy for social media and Google Ads, tips and tricks on writing the best ad copy for your software application*; and *examples of ads* that I think possess captivating copy.

We shall also take some time to talk a little about how to create some of the more consistent, text-based parts of your brand.

Outside of the name of your company and/or software application, you will also want to, as a part of your ad copy and overall branding, create tagline(s), slogans, motto(s), etc.

These are typically simple but self-explanatory and work very well with your brand to let users and potential users know what you stand for. We shall also look at some of my favorite taglines and slogans from other companies.

**Generally speaking**

The term "Ad copy" refers to the text, whether written or audible, any marketing campaign or advertising contains.

This is the "words" part of an advertisement. Throughout many Ad houses in America and the world over, a lot of attention is paid to the words any brand chooses to use in their advertising.

This is super important as your ad copy, especially on social media, will be the main engine that drives conversion, which will determine the number of visits you get to your landing pages, which influences how many folks sign up for your trial, and so on. You get the picture.

## Good copy sells

Even more consequential  than the videos and images you use in your ads, especially on social media, "good", captivating, effective, ad copy will be the thing that tells your brand story and speaks to your audience directly.

With platforms like Facebook and Google - via their new and improved iteration of their Google Ads platform, you will be able to specifically target folks all around the world, based on any number of specifications you can think of.

## Especially on Facebook

Despite all the hoopla made every day about the fading power of Facebook, I still find the social media giant to be eternally useful when it comes to digital advertising. I mean, there is no denying that when it comes to social media advertising, Facebook is truly the 800-pound gorilla in the room. Facebook, by far is still the most used social media platform. Since its launch in 2004, the user base for the social behemoth has only grown.

The site, if we can still call it that, is used by *2.5 billion people on a monthly basis* - The coveted "active user" measure. And since only *48% of Facebook Ad revenue comes from the United States and Canada*, you have a tremendous opportunity to be able to reach audiences all over the.

*94% of Facebook Ad revenue is from mobile and the average cost per click for a Facebook Ad is $1.72.*

Hopefully, I have been able to accomplish the goal of trying to show you the potential you have to make a big impact with your SaaS by choosing Facebook as one of your main advertising channels.

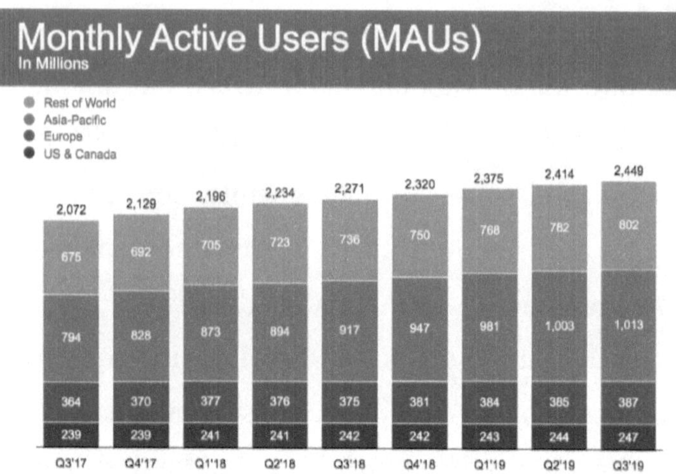



## Google Advertising works too

Being the O.G of online advertising, and still going strong after all these years, Google for me is still a strong contender in the online advertising space. At our firm, Corvus Web Services, we actually use three main advertising channels.

We use Google, Facebook, and do some onboarding and product announcements via email marketing. These are the only types of marketing outreach we do. Google Ads can be a bit pricey, especially when starting out but will eventually become one of your biggest drivers of quality user growth.

By design, Google Ads will especially help you reach folks all over the world who are specifically looking for what you are selling. This unique difference between Google and Social media ads is the reason I, among many other software entrepreneurs I speak to, use both types of platforms to help boost their online advertising efforts.

By using Google as one of your sales and marketing avenues, you will also have a chance to dip your toe into the highly effective world of video advertising through YouTube Ads. Now, full disclosure: We don't do a whole lot of YouTube ad-ing at our firm. We plan to start soon, and maybe I will be able to speak a little more intelligently about it down the line. I must say though that we have seen some impressive conversion numbers based on the few (temporary) YouTube ads we have tried.

That being said, Google ads are still as important today as they were about twenty years ago. Most folks start looking for stuff online first by going to Google to perform a search. This is where all or most online activity starts. Get this, 3.5 billion searches are made every day on Google. 90% of searches made on desktops are done via Google.

These are really important metrics to keep in mind as you create ads for your software application. Especially if you are in the business-to-business space. Business apps would be apps like Salesforce, Hubspot, and Slack. These are tools used by serious businesspeople and are therefore accessed mostly via desktops and other business devices.

As you ponder the prospect of launching Google ads, you should also know that:

- 35% of product searches start on Google.

- Organic Google results with 3-4 words in the title drive higher CTRs than organic results with 1-2 words in the title.

- 52% of global internet traffic comes from mobile devices.

- Google captures 95% of the mobile search engine market in the U.S

- 42% of mobile-driven brand interactions involve Google search.

## A Compelling story

Getting back to the man topic of discussion. You must keep these various differences between Google Ads and social media ads in mind as your procced to think about, or write quality copy for your ads. You must also remember some of the stats we looked at and create ads that speak directly to your audience, tell your full brand story, and deliver a precise message to the folks you want to reach regardless of their geographic location. For the purpose of the next few sections, I shall focus on Facebook and Google Ads. I will also again use Mango as our example as I walk you through some of the ways to write quality ad copy or your SaaS campaign(s).

## A one-way conversation

Writing ad copy for Google ads is totally dissimilar to copy for Facebook ads. For starters, each platform has their own unique way of combining other brand assets with text to form the total structure of their ads. For Google, assuming that you will start with text-based ads, you will have plenty of opportunities to communicate with your audience since these types of ads tend to allow plenty of room for text.

For Facebook ads, you will be able to create detailed descriptions and compelling titles. But for the most part, these types of ads lean hard on more visual elements to communicate your message. Either way, you will want to adhere to these essential tips when creating copy for your Google and/or Facebook ads.

## Speak directly to your audience

It is important that you refrain from using hyperbole when writing copy. Trust me when I tell you that these types of ads are often perceived as dubious and salesy. Instead, I encourage you to try to create a vibe of having kind of a one-on-one conversation with your audience.

Try to specifically address any pain point(s) your potential user might have which led them to search for yours and other products like yours in the first place.

Try something like:

*"Looking for a contact management solution that won't break the bank?"*,

or

*"Mango is a contact management solution for non-techie entrepreneurs"*

**Use Keywords**

We have talked a bit about how important it is to use Google's Keyword research tools, or any other set of keyword analysis tools like SEMrush or Alexa, to gauge the popularity of a group of keywords and phrases as it relates to your Software-as-a-service platform.

Armed with your new set of synthesized keywords, you will be able to position your ads to attract the maximum amount of traffic if you use the most relevant keywords and phrase throughout your social media and Google Ads.

I am sure you have noticed other brands do this. This is especially important when also trying to score some great placements in organic search results as well.

I will however caution that you do not over do this. Try to, in your headlines and the description of your Facebook and Google Ads, use relevant keywords and key phrases in the most natural ways possible. Try to be as specific in your use of keywords as possible. And try to be sure to use keywords that are highly relevant to the landing page the user will be taken to when they click on your ad or search result(s).

**Match Ad copy with visuals**

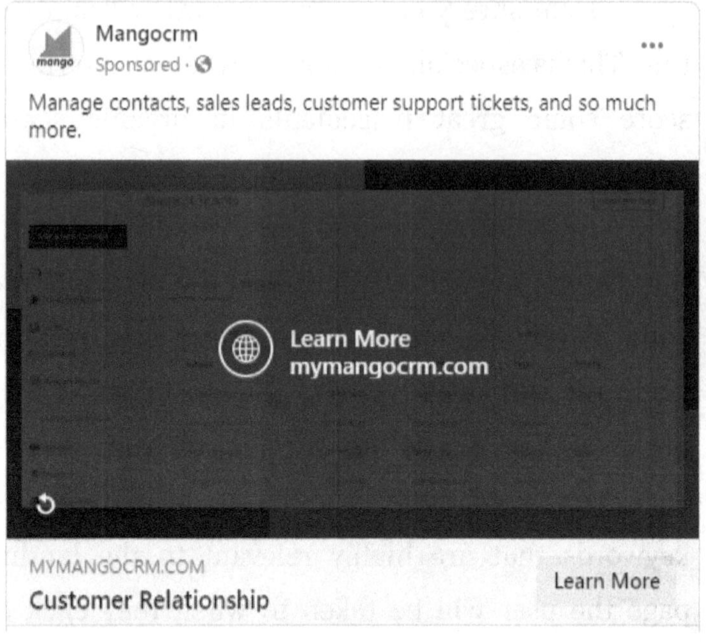


Your ads will, and should speak directly to your audience. Emphasis on "speak". With this in mind, you will want to, for maximum conversion, communicate fully with every aspect of your campaign infrastructure. Your images, videos, landing pages, etc. Must all tell the same story. Folks should be able to, by just looking at any part of your ad, have an idea what you are offering.

## A targeted audience

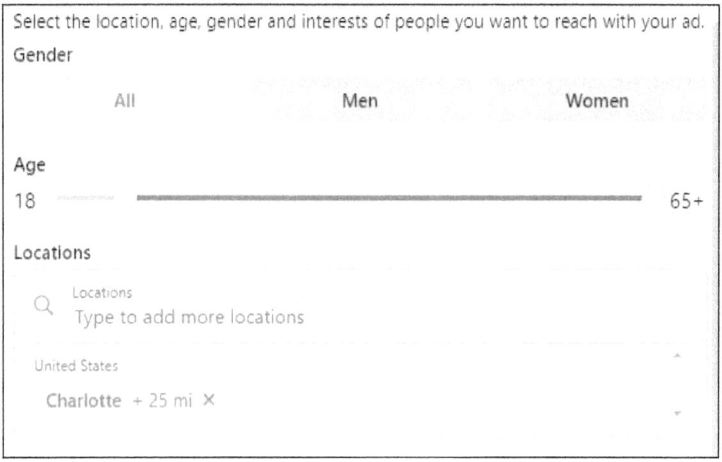

Select the location, age, gender and interests of people you want to reach with your ad.

Gender

All            Men            Women

Age

18 ——————————————————————————— 65+

Locations

Locations
Type to add more locations

United States

Charlotte  + 25 mi  ✕

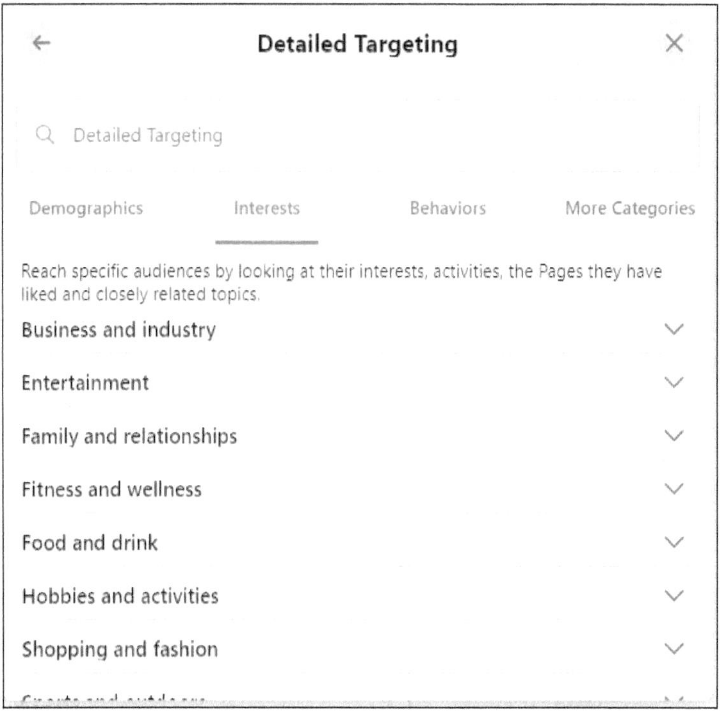

---

← **Detailed Targeting** ✕

Detailed Targeting

Demographics        Interests        Behaviors        More Categories

Reach specific audiences by looking at their interests, activities, the Pages they have liked and closely related topics.

Business and industry                          ⌄

Entertainment                                  ⌄

Family and relationships                       ⌄

Fitness and wellness                           ⌄

Food and drink                                 ⌄

Hobbies and activities                         ⌄

Shopping and fashion                           ⌄

One of the awesome things about Facebook marketing is the specificity with which you can target potential users. Armed with all the demographics tools the Facebook ad platform has to offer, you can build multiple ads to target each group of potential users you wish to reach.

For starters, you can target folks as near as your locality- city or town, and as far as the other side of the globe. You can also find users for your app based on their interests, professional backgrounds, education, and even based on other apps they like. I invite you to set up a page for your app on Facebook and play around with their ad interface a bit to get the hang of it.

## Show value

If you have read any of my books, you probably have picked up on how much I talk about "value" and "Presenting value".

I am always going on and on about the need for entrepreneurs to show value in their products and services. In SaaS, value is to be seen not shown. What this means is that you must craft your ads based on an app that shows obvious value.

Users must be able to clearly see the value your app holds (for them) based on your ads and your software application as well. Intrinsic value is especially important in the subscription space since your paid subscribers will need to see ongoing value in your app to justify the monthly payments coming out of their accounts.

I am sure you have built an application chock full of features that provide value to your users. I am sure your design and product development apparatus took care of that part. When it comes to your ads, be short and sweet, and above all else, state your value in your ads.

Description
MangoCRM is a Contact management for the rest of us. Add Unlimited users for $9/mo. No annual contracts. No hidden fees. No complications. Manage your business billing, contacts, leads, and more with Mango.

## Test as a much as you can

It goes without saying that when it comes to sales and marketing, there is no one sure way to do things. This part of the process is more art than science. I can only share insights on some of the

Things I have done and the ways in which I have done them that have amounted to some degree of success. I encourage you to try some of these techniques as I share them. However, you will be able to zero in on what works best for your app if you create various types of ads, deploy them and see which ones get you the conversions and upgrades you seek.

# CHAPTER SIX

# SLOGANS & TAGLINES

Slogans and taglines, and to some extent, even mottos, are meant to express complex and often multifaceted concepts in simple terms. Admittedly this whole idea may seem oxymoronic, and yet that is exactly what they are meant to represent: Concise expressions of complex ideas and concepts.

Most iconic brands have adopted slogans and taglines for their overall companies, and oftentimes even for their individual products and services. Companies like P&G are in the habit of rolling out full advertising and branding packages for each of the many products they make and market.

We, as consumers typically recognize popular slogans and taglines; and are able to associate them with specific services and/or products almost instantly. We have all grown accustomed to identifying brands and products based on, among other things, their slogans and taglines.

*"A 15-minute call could save you 15% on car insurance"*.

I am sure these words mean something to you, right?

## One or the other

Although some use the words "slogan" and "tagline" interchangeably, there are significant differences between them. For one, slogans tend to tell a much more vivid story of what a company does, how it does it, and who it does it for. Meaning, its commitment to its customers, users, shareholders, and so on. For these reasons, slogans are often longer and more robust.

Taglines, on the other hand, are meant to be short and catchy. They are meant to be used to help users, and potential customers build an affinity for the company, brand, or product.

Often written below a company's logo on marketing materials, taglines are meant to create brand awareness and a feel for the way a company communicates with its customers as part of its broader brand identity.

Applebees for example, via their "Eatin' Good in the Neighborhood." Slogan wants all to know that they are the place around the corner you can go to grab a bite - With, or without your family and friends. No fancy stuff, simply good food. At least that is what I get out of the slogan.

**Only the best slogans**

Dunkin' Donuts: "America Runs on Dunkin'", Nike: "Just do it", Apple: "Think Different." These are all highly memorable slogans and taglines. And with good reason. There are various strategies that go into writing great slogans and taglines.

If you are not only building one Software application, but hope, and plan to build a business around your SaaS application(s), you will want to consider the following tips to help come up with a slogan and tagline that both represent your app and overall brand:

**Memorable** A "good" slogan, or tagline is one that people remember and can easily associate with your brand. Be sure to create slogans, especially for your app, that speaks to the types of people who will use your platform. If your app is meant to reach a creative, artsy audience, be sure to use language that represents the views and beliefs of those among us who express themselves in creative, beautiful ways. If your SaaS platform will be used by salespeople, go out of your way to craft your slogans and taglines to speak to these types of results-oriented people.

**Positive vibes:** This is one of those tips that seems obvious. But in the midst of intense competition, some brands may wonder into the dark when it comes to their brand identity. Try to resist the temptation to go negative when it comes to your slogans and taglines. No jabbing at the competition, or anyone else for that matter. Keep it light and positive at all times.

**Unique quotes**: Uniqueness is one of the most powerful marketing tools there is. Especially in the crowded world of SaaS. With billions of software applications out there, it is impossible to create an app dissimilar in every way from one that is already on the market. You can, however, present your solution(s) in a way that is unlike any other. Keep this concept in mind as you write your taglines and slogans.

Be sure to communicate your uniqueness every chance you get. I am big fan of Slack, the team communication tool. The company is rumored to have an unofficial slogan of *"Work hard and go home."*

To me, the firm finds ways to differentiate its offerings by appealing to the workaholics in some of us. Are there other communications tools out there like Slack? Sure! Even ones that predate it.

Slack, however, lets the world know that their app is not for "Slackers". This is not your momma's chat tool. This is for folks who work in teams and they work hard. So, work hard and go home!

**Short and sweet:** This one is pretty self-explanatory. I will reiterate this point though. Throughout your marketing for your software app, you will get plenty of chances to tell full stories about what your software does, what your company is all about, and so on. When it comes to your slogans and taglines though, it is imperative that you keep it short so as to maintain the type of memorability we discussed earlier.

**Benefits and all:** A key step to take when crafting slogans and taglines, in my opinion, is to simply tell folks what your software does as part of your slogan. *"We make work, work"*. *"Contact management for the rest of us"*. Something like that. A great slogan does well to not tout a list of features, but to clearly communicate the benefit(s) a user can expect to derive from the product or service.

**Famous Examples**

*Maybelline*: *"Maybe she's born with it. Maybe it's Maybelline."*

**Audi:** *"Advancement Through Technology"*

**L'Oréal Paris**: *"Because You're Worth It."*

## Inspiration

*-Logoorbit.com*

*Software for the Open Enterprise*

*People Making Technology Work*

*Wireless Made Simple*

*A Virtual World of Live Pictures.*

*You've got questions, we've got answers*

*Technology for Innovators*

*Your potential. Our passion.*

*A magical and revolutionary device at an unbelievable price.*


*Has it Changed Your Life Yet?*

# CHAPTER SEVEN

# COST OF DOING BUSINESS

As you may well know, sales and marketing, or rather the act of "selling stuff" is about as old as time itself. I am sure that Ovid himself would agree that (probably) even before the iron ages, our ancestors were most likely, on the plains of north Africa, going from cave to cave trying to sell/barter things like animal skins and horns with one another.

We sell. This is what we do. Over time, as markets have become crowded, we as humans have had to find new ways to reach those, we seek to sell our goods and services to.

The Digital age, as it were, has undoubtedly brought about many advancements in the ways in which we reach our prospective customers.

Today, customers all around the world are being reached via social media marketing, Television ads, text messaging, and so on. One thing remains the same though.

To reach a wider audience, one must take unprecedented steps and spend some time and money in order to get our "stuff" in front of as many people as possible.

I invite you, as a software entrepreneur, to keep these concepts in mind as this is one of those types of realities that folks starting out in SaaS OFTEN ignore.

Sure, if you have a great and unique app, and as a result manage to instantly rank high on natural search, then you will probably not need to spend much if any on marketing. We saw software tools like Salesforce, Netflix, and Yahoo Mail take markets by storm simply because they were the first of their kind.

Until the launch of Netflix's streaming service, folks had no idea watching movies online as part of a monthly subscription was even a thing.

These types of "first mover" tools are able to gain almost instant popularity due to the newness and the uniqueness of their offerings. Makers of these types of tools, in these types of unique situations often only have to engage in some good old-fashioned P.R for the world to take notice.

For the rest of us, we must carefully plan out a paid marketing campaign(s). We must endeavor to stretch our often-limited financial resources in ways that allow us to deploy as many effective marketing campaigns for our SaaS app while maintaining a healthy level of cash reserves. A challenge that often leads to the performance of various balancing acts.

How do we do this? This is partly the reason I wrote this book to begin with. As I close things out, I would like to take this final chapter to go over some of the points to consider as part of your budgeting process for "marketing and advertising" for your SaaS platform.

*Publius Ovidius Naso, known as Ovid in the English-speaking world, was a Roman poet who lived during the reign of Augustus. He was a contemporary of the older Virgil and Horace, with whom he is often ranked as one of the three canonical poets of Latin literature.*

## Setting goals

As a matter of fact, there is very little that can deliberately be accomplished without goals and objectives. These must be established, I believe, at the outset of any undertaking if any level of success is to be expected.

This is a crucial initial step for your Software marketing campaign. You must start with goals. What do you hope to accomplish/ get out of this first specific marketing campaign?

I find that I am best served when I provide clear answers to the following questions as part of my marketing goal-setting process.

## How much do I have to spend?

The answer to this question will obviously vary from person to person, situation to situation. Although, I have found that it is best to establish a strict budget for each group of ads or marketing campaigns.

Some marketing initiatives will be based on a rollout of a beta. Others will depend on some new feature you are introducing. Or perhaps a seasonal campaign.

Either way, it is important that you dedicate a finite level of financial resources to help get the word out. It is important, for the overall financial health of your business, that you stick to your planned budget.

It is also crucial that you decide how much cash to dedicate towards which advertising platforms, and what each ad is meant to accomplish.

**Which platforms I will advertise with?**
Which brings us to the next question. It is key that you take the time to carefully research which advertising channels work best for you app. If you are rolling out a business software tool, then you will want to add Google Advertising and LinkedIn to your set of marketing platforms.

The use of email will also aid you greatly as a way to reach out to new potential users, and to onboard your trial and paid users. At our firm, we have found (as I mentioned earlier) that Facebook Ads really work well to tell folks around the world about any new Software-as-a-service offerings we roll out.

With Facebook, we are able to micro-target and reach folks based on all sorts of permutations, at a fraction of the cost it would require with other social media platforms. We have also been experimenting with Quora for business lately.

Try to determine which mix of social media platforms will work best with your app.

Once you have been able to select which channels you will use to market your app. I implore you to exercise discipline and stick with these platforms to allow for maximum results. Try not to go down the rabbit hole of checking out every single new shiny social media platform that comes out. You are sure to waste valuable marketing dollars this way.

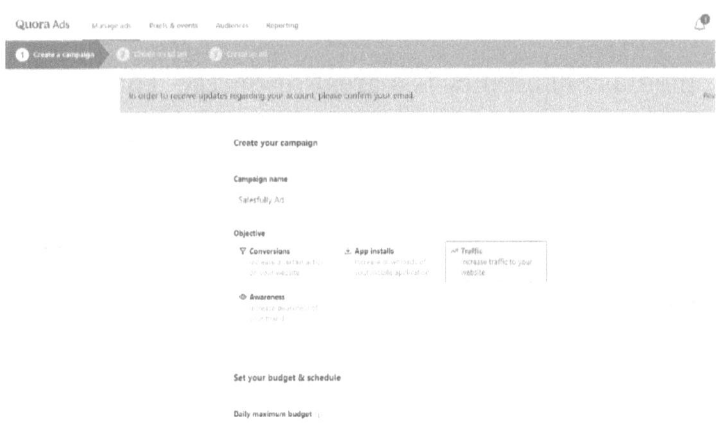

## What types of content will I use?

As I am sure you have figured out by now that when it comes to marketing, especially online, the type of content used in ads makes a huge difference as it relates to engagement. We stand to illicit various levels of responses to our campaigns based on the types of text, images, and videos we choose to use.

The great thing about digital marketing, among other things, is how accurately we can measure results.

Due to this level of accuracy, we as entrepreneurs are able to tap into an existing treasure trove of data to guide us when we are at the stage where we need to determine which types of content to use for our digital marketing initiatives.

I always find myself looking for relevant, timely data to help in the area. Buffer, the social media consultancy is a great resource - They seem to invest a tremendous amount of resources in compiling, analyzing, and making these kinds of datapoint available for free on their website (www.buffer.com/resources).

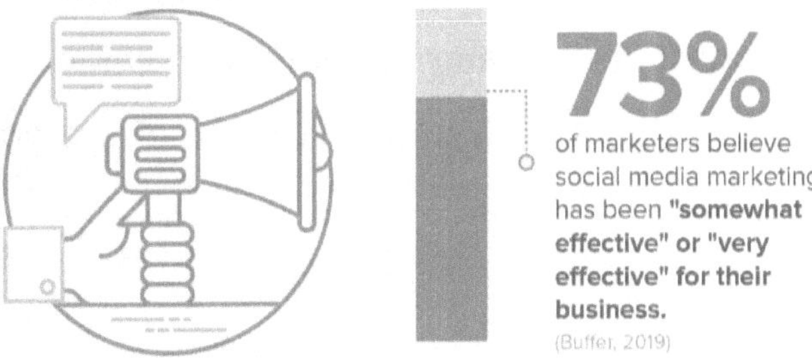


## What will success look like?

At what point will you seek to consider your specific marketing campaign a success? Well, this depends on what the goal of your campaign was and what type of campaign this was. With some various goals and examples of campaign types, you will be able to definitively tell if you were able to hit your proposed benchmarks.

For example, did you want to be able to sign up your first 100 free trial users when you launched your limited beta campaign on Facebook? If so, how much were you looking to spend to do so?

And were you able to, or plan to engage in some creative onboarding to try to extract some valuable feedback to use to build-out the rest of your line of features?

These are some of the things to consider when you think about "points of success" and what comes next once you are able to accomplish some of the goals you set out for your ads.

## What comes next?

So, what comes next? What will you do once you accomplish, or fail to hit the goals you set out for your SaaS marketing campaign?

Well, before we look at that, let me throw in one other factor: Time, right? You will have to give your ads time to percolate through the interwebs, right?

So, once you have applied your budget, and time – enough time to know whether your campaign has served its purpose or not, what comes next?

What we try to do is replicate various elements of a successful campaign to be used in future ads. We stick to the types of ad copy, images, videos, etc. That work well. This is a practice that I encourage a lot when I talk to other entrepreneurs and marketers. In business, you always want to retain, replicate, and maximize on the things that WORK.

For unsuccessful campaigns, depending on the type of campaigns we ran, we try to get feedback from those that saw our ads, and/or signed up for atrial but did not complete all the steps we set forth to see how we can either improve our messaging, app, or both.

**That being said**

I hope you have enjoyed this book. I look forward to any comments or feedback you may have for me.

You can reach me by visiting

www.ostrichpress.com.

# Thank you!

# Notes

*https://optinmonster.com/video-marketing-statistics-what-you-must-know/*

*https://www.semrush.com/login/*

*https://www.marketingsherpa.com/article/case-study/tigerfitness-content-marketing-strategy*

*https://www.tigerfitness.com/blogs/tools/free-workout-plan-1*

*https://gs.statcounter.com/search-engine-market-share*

*https://unbounce.com/*

*https://www.leadpages.net/pricing*

*https://thrivehive.com/benefits-landing-pages/*

*https://ads.google.com/aw/keywordplanner/ideas/new?ocid=270605976&euid=281812230&__u=1248733270&uscid=270605976&__c=3079153624&authuser=2&subid=ww-ww-et-g-aw-a-vasquette_ads_1%21o2*

*https://blog.hubspot.com/marketing/brand-slogans-and-taglines*

*https://thebrandboy.com/best-slogans-for-software-company/*

https://www.logoorbit.com/industry/technology/techn
ology-slogans

https://www.amazon.com/SEO-2019-optimization-
marketing-strategies-
ebook/dp/B00NH0XZR0/ref=sr_1_1_sspa?dchild=1
&keywords=seo&qid=1591874980&s=digital-
text&sr=1-1-
spons&psc=1&spLa=ZW5jcnlwdGVkUXVhbGlmaW
VyPUFEWTFDWkRVVDNDM0cmZW5jcnlwdGVkS
WQ9QTA2Mzk2OTgxN0RDWEFMT0xFU1lEJmVuY
3J5cHRlZEFkSWQ9QTAxNzcxNDczQlU5NEwwQ0
M5WDIzJndpZGdldE5hbWU9c3BfYXRmJmFjdGlvbj
1jbGlja1JlZGlyZWN0JmRvTm90TG9nQ2xpY2s9dH
J1ZQ==

https://www.wordstream.com/blog/ws/2016/06/29/be
st-facebook-ads

https://www.wordstream.com/blog/ws/2015/04/21/ad
words-ads
https://sproutsocial.com/insights/facebook-stats-for-
marketers/#:~:text=5.,use%20the%20site%20every
%20day.

*https://www.emarketer.com/content/more-product-searches-start-on-amazon*

*https://www.wordstream.com/blog/ws/2019/02/07/google-search-statistics*

*https://www.statista.com/statistics/216573/worldwide-market-share-of-search-engines/*

*https://blog.hubspot.com/marketing/local-seo-stats*

*https://www.smartinsights.com/search-engine-optimisation-seo/seo-analytics/comparison-of-google-clickthrough-rates-by-position/*

*https://www.quora.com/q/quoraforbusiness*

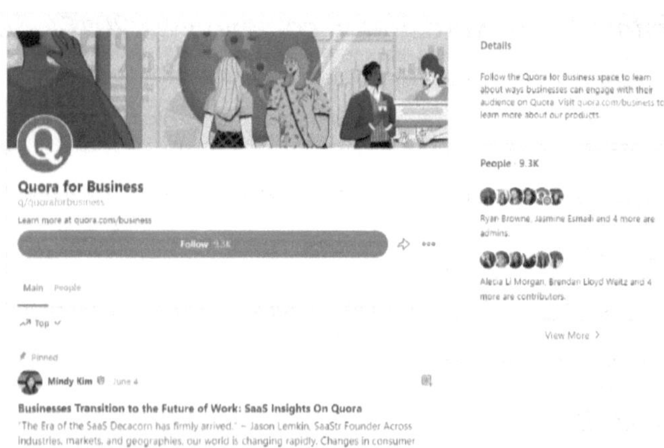

*https://buffer.com/analyze?utm_source=resources&utm_medium=blog&utm_campaign=analyze-launch&utm_content=social-media-stats*

*https://buffer.com/resources/social-media-stats*

# About the Author

*Frank Dappah* is an entrepreneur and the author of over 15 business and sales books as well as various kid titles. Through OSTRICH PUBLISHERS, an independent publishing company he founded with his wife, he has published popular sales titles as The Telesales Handbook, Startup Monday, and others.

# Author's other books

**Payment Received: Learn how to successfully launch your Software-as-a-service platform.**

Payment Received is one of the best books on SaaS pricing and marketing. In this easy-to-follow book, I lay out a few strategies on how to successfully bring your software-as-a-service or subscription-based app to market.

## STATUS UPDATE

# STATUS UPDATE

## How to generate and convert health and life insurance sales leads with Facebook Ads

### FRANK DAPPAH

Small business social media marketing guide

Strategic social media marketing can be the cure-all your business needs to reach the right audience at the right time. STATUS UPDATE is an easy-to-digest guide to help any Life and/or Health agent or agency make the most of their Facebook marketing system.

**Startup Monday: How to tackle some of the often-overlooked challenges you will face while trying to grow your Startup company**

# STARTUP

HOW TO TACKLE SOME OF THE OFTEN OVERLOOKED CHALLENGES THAT YOU WILL FACE WHILE GROWING YOUR STARTUP

# MONDAY

## FRANK DAPPAH

Startup Monday is an easy-to-digest, straight-to-the-point book about Leadership, growth, and corporate culture. This 160-plus page book is my latest attempt at helping any entrepreneur or business owner out there, based on my own personal experiences, navigate the unique set of challenges one faces when trying to grow a Startup company that has started ..

To review more of Frank's books, please
visit www.ostrichpress.com

OSTRICH PUBLISHERS

---

# Books

*Browse the latest book releases from our Authors*

**New Release**

## HOW I BUILT MY SUCCESSFUL HEALTH INSURANCE AGENCY WITH OBAMACARE PLANS

*Learn How To Build A Health Insurance Business One Client at A Time*

BUY NOW

## How to be a Successful Insurance Agent

AN INSURANCE AGENT'S GUIDE TO PROSPECTING AND CLOSING SALES

Are you an Insurance Agent looking for help closing more sales? This is the ideal guide to help you become efficient at uncovering prospective customers and conducting appointments that close more sales.

BUY NOW

## PERSONA: A Step-by-step Guide to Identifying and Attracting Profitable Customers to Your New Business

A must-read for new business owners and Entrepreneurs just getting started.

BUY NOW

## ADVENTURES IN MARKETING AUTOMATION

Adventures in Marketing Automation is a simple but comprehensive guide on how any small business owner or entrepreneur can use the power of social media, email, SMS, and other tools to help automate their entire marketing systems. All in an effort to grow a more efficient and profitable business.

BUY NOW

## PIXIE DUST: How to Convince Investors to Invest in Your Business

This is an opportunity to learn how to attract investors to your business. Learn how to position yourself and your company or business idea to attract Angel Investors and/or Venture Capital Investors. Learn how to produce quality pitch decks, Elegant Elevator pitches, and so much more.

BUY NOW

# Our mission

OSTRICH is an all-digital publisher. Our mission is to create a robust medium through which talented independent Authors and Creatives can share their works with the rest of the world.

## What we do

As part of our overall mission, we work closely with authors of all backgrounds to help bring their works to life.

Through our robust distribution infrastructure, we can help Authors, who would otherwise go unnoticed, to plan, create and distribute their finished products worldwide.

We work with Authors at every step of the process, from brainstorming, to writing, to distribution and marketing. We are working hard to build an all-inclusive publishing and distribution platform.

OSTRICH™

ISBN: 9798655780798

Cover and Interior design: Ostrich Publishers



This novel is a work of fiction. Any references to real people, events, establishments, organizations, and locales are intended only to give the fiction a sense of reality and authenticity. Other characters, names, places, and incidents portrayed herein are either the product of the author's imagination or are used fictitiously.

Printed in The United States of America

# ANOTHER

A GREAT GUIDE FOR ASPIRING
SOFTWARE ENTREPRENEURS

SOFTWARE AS A SERVICE

# MARKETING

USEFUL TIPS AND TRICKS TO HELP YOU
MARKET YOUR SOFTWARE APPLICATION

# BOOK

FRANK DAPPAH

www.ingramcontent.com/pod-product-compliance
Lightning Source LLC
Chambersburg PA
CBHW021001180726
47993CB00017B/530